Introduction

This is a book about listening which will help you prepare for the listening section of the GCSE music examination. It will also help you to realise what a lot more you can get out of music by listening harder. Many of the exercises will give you practice in matching sound to sign and sign to sound. Others will draw your attention to what the music is trying to say and the way it is saying it.

Examples are drawn from a wide range of style and period including folk, rock, jazz, vocal, instrumental and chamber music, as well as music for brass bands and other groups. Some of the synthesised techniques used in the world of pop and rock music are also covered.

The book has four levels each of which ends with two tests. These will help you to gain experience in the way you approach a real test. Each level has five sections:

Beats and bars, as it names suggests, is about rhythm.

Shapes and sizes lets you listen to the way a tune grows from melodic shapes made up from steps, jumps and repeated notes. It also demonstrates the effect of some intervals like octaves and 5ths.

Chords and cadences deals with sounds which occur when more than one note at a time is played and sung. It also gives you practice in recognising the way music is punctuated with cadences.

Groups and families lets you hear instruments and voices by themselves and together. It will help you to become aware of the sound of various combinations and of their different textures.

Light and shade is about soft and loud, broken and smooth sounds and other instrumental and electronic effects.

There will be plenty of time to listen and complete the exercises so try not to panic. Listen hard and concentrate and your aural ability will develop. You will not only find that you can pass the examination, but also that you enjoy and appreciate all kinds of music even more.

Level 1

Beats and bars 1

So many good rhythms are really very simple. Sometimes they are just made up of crotchets and quavers with perhaps a few rests.

1 Listen to this four-bar phrase played on a snare drum.

Notice that when the drum remains silent for a beat, a one-beat or crotchet rest is inserted.

    Now listen to the same rhythm shared between a snare and bass drum. Complete the pattern adding one beat rests where necessary. Notice that in bar 3 the snare drum does not play at all so a whole bar rest is used.

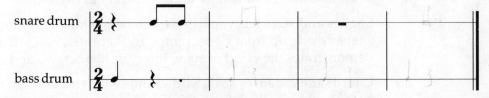

2 The next example is also four bars long, but there are more than two beats in each bar. Can you hear how many?

    Listen again: bar 3 contains a different pattern from bars 1, 2 and 4. Look at the three patterns below and copy out the correct pattern for bar 3.

Listen Around

**Geoffrey Winters and
Jim Northfield**

Contents

Level 1
Level 2
Level 3
Level 4

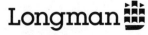

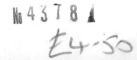

A Teacher's Book and a cassette accompany this book
Other titles in the GCSE Music Skills series
Listen, Compose, Perform   **by Geoffrey Winters**
Composing   **by Martin Hinckley**

Acknowledgements

We are grateful to the following for permission to reproduce music
copyright material:
English Folk Dance & Song Society for tunes to 'My Love She's but a
Lassie Yet', 'Dorset four-hand reel', 'The old grey cat', 'Gilderoy', tune
& words to 'Blow the man down bullies' from *Community Dances
Manuals* (c) EDFSS; International Music Publications for eight bars
rhythm from 'Sweet Adeline' by Harry Armstrong & Richard Gerard
(c) 1903 M. Witmark & Sons USA. Sub-pubd by B. Feldman & Co. Ltd,
London WC2H OLD. Reproduced by permission of EMI Music Pubg
& IMP; Oxford University Press for tunes to 'Linstead Market' & 'Wata
come a me y'eye' from *Folk Songs of Jamaica* collected by Tom Murray (c)
1952; R. Smith & Co. Ltd, Watford, England for melodic excerpts from
The Galloping Major by G. Bastow/F. Jacob, transcr. G. Brand,
Bandutopia by R. Farnon & 'On the trail' from *The Golden West* by S.
Johnson; United Music Publishers Ltd/Editions Alphonse Leduc, Paris
for an extract from the flute part of Ibert *Deux Interludes* No.2; Universal
Edition (London) Ltd for bars 172-175-cello part & bars 179-181-violin
part, bars 196-199-violin part from Paul Patterson's *String Quartet* 2nd
movement and bars 5-12-trombone part from Kodály *Háry János* fourth
movement.
We have unfortunately been unable to trace the copyright holders of
'Gathering up the Roses in the Wild Wood' and would appreciate any
information that would enable us to do so.
The copyright work by Ibert (*Deux Interludes*) No.2 is specifically
excluded from any blanket photocopy arrangements.

3   The next rhythm is played on a bass drum, snare drum and a third percussion instrument. Listen carefully to the piece and complete the notation for all three instruments, adding one- and two-beat rests where necessary.

snare drum

bass drum

Which instrument played the third percussion part: a cymbal, a woodblock or a triangle?

4   Listen again to example 1. Compare it with the next example. In this some of the notes have been joined or tied together. Can you hear the effect of the first note lasting into the second beat of the bar?

Here is a neater way of writing the same rhythm.

The dot after the first beat replaces the tied half-beat or quaver.

The following two-bar phrases each include a ♩. ♪ rhythm. Listen to the recording and decide where it occurs. Add a dot after the crotchet which is lengthened and a tail to the next note to turn it into a quaver.

Shapes and sizes 1

A tune may have a number of melodic shapes.
Some shapes move up or down a note at a time.

Some jump across several steps in one go.

Others stop on one note just like a rhythm.

The different melodic shapes all help to give the tune its character.

1 Here are three sets of melodic shapes which move up or down a step at a
time. Listen to the recording and then copy out the shape in each set
which matches the music.

2 The difference in pitch between two sounds is called an interval. When
measuring the size of an interval include both the lower and higher
sounds. The interval between two next door notes, like D and E, is a 2nd.
Few tunes move just in 2nds. Most mix these steps with jumps and
repeated notes to give them character and variety.

(a) In the carol tune *The First Nowell*, it is quite a long time before there is
a jump.
Copy out the words, think through the tune in your head and then
put a line between the two words where the jump occurs.

The first Nowell the angel did say
Was to certain poor shepherds in fields as they lay;

(b) Now do the same with *My Grandfather's Clock.*
This has three jumps and some repeated notes. As often happens, the first jump comes right at the beginning.

My grandfather's clock was too tall for the shelf
So it stood ninety years on the floor.

Can you mark where the repeated notes come?

3   Here are the bar plans of three tunes which have several repeated notes. Copy the plans, then listen to the recording. When you have decided which bars include repeated notes, show them by writing their rhythm in crotchets and quavers, or by marking the bar with an R.

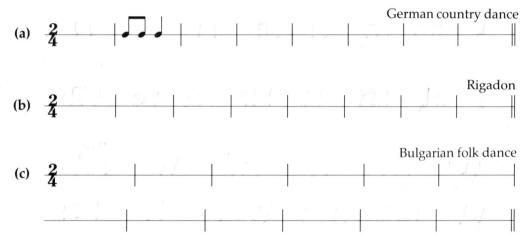

In the last tune there were three jumps. Can you find them?

4   Listen to the next tune, which dates from the middle of the 19th century when there was a terrible potato famine in Ireland. Put a circle round the words which are set to this shape.

Oh the praties they grow small,
Over here, over here;
Oh the praties they grow small and we dig them in the fall,
And we eat them skins and all,
Over here, over here.

5 The tune of *Good King Wenceslas* is largely stepwise with just a few jumps and repeated notes. Think of the tune in your head and then complete the notation of the music.

Good King Wen-ces - las looked out   On the   feast of   Ste - phen,

When the snow lay   round a - bout,   Deep and crisp and   e - ven:

Bright-ly shone the moon that night,   Though the frost was   cru - el,

When a poor man   came in sight   Gath'ring win-ter   fu ——— - el.

Chords and cadences 1

1 Here is the notation of the Bulgarian folk dance to which you have just listened. You will be able to see where the repeated notes and jumps came. Did you find them all?

Now listen to the tune played in three different ways. Choose from the

boxes below the best description of each.

in the wrong rhythm	with long, low held sounds	jerky and hard

sweetly, with an extra part	high and shrill	very noisily

2   In the last example, the Bulgarian folk dance was accompanied by a drone in the bass. Here are four kinds of drones. Try and imagine what they sound like. Now listen to the recording and say which kind of drone is used for each piece. Can you recognise any of the instruments which play?

As in the examples you have just heard, a drone may be just a single note which is held on or repeated, or it may be an interval like a fifth or an octave. The two notes of the interval may be played at the same time or one after the other.

3   Perfect 5ths and octaves have a clear, pure sound which stands out from the sound of other intervals.

a   Listen to the recording of six intervals, 1, 2, 3, 4, 5, 6. Pick out the perfect 5ths. There are two of them.

b   Listen to the recording of another six intervals. Pick out the two octaves. Because an octave has two notes of the same name, it may sound almost like a single note instead of an interval.

4   **a**   The harpsichord piece with a drone is about 'buffoons, jugglers and rope-dancers with bears and monkeys'. It is by François Couperin who wrote many descriptive pieces. It is a dance in triple time and is made up of 2- and 4-bar phrases. Listen to it again and make a plan of its phrase structure which starts with two 4-bar phrases like this:

| 4 | 4 | ? | ? | and so on.

   b   Some tunes, like *Good King Wenceslas*, have a longer phrase somewhere. Look back and find out where its phrases begin and end, then draw a plan of the structure.

   c   More unusually, the Bulgarian folk dance is not built from 2- and 4-bar phrases. Look and listen to it again and then make a plan showing its phrase structure.

5   Sometimes a short phrase is passed from one instrument or group to another. This antiphonal treatment is a feature of barber-shop singing where a solo voice is answered by the whole group. Listen to part of *Sweet Adeline*. Follow the rhythm printed below and then rewrite it on two lines for solo and grouped voices. Do not forget to add rests where necessary.

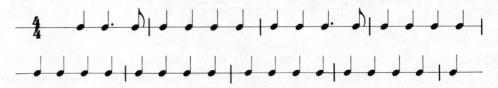

6   Sometimes the notes of a melody are doubled with the same sounds an octave higher or lower.

Mozart K455

Sometimes other notes are added to give a richer texture in harmony.

Listen to the recording and notice the changes in texture. Write out the bar numbers 1 to 16 and put a circle round all those that are played in harmony instead of in octaves.

Groups and families 1

Have you ever played the word association game where someone says a word and you respond with the first thing that comes into your head?

What would be your response to the word 'keyboard'? Piano perhaps? Organ? Synthesiser or Harpsichord? Any of these would be correct because the word 'keyboard' can represent a whole group or family of instruments which have something in common, in this case the arrangement of black and white notes which are struck by the performer.

1 Listen carefully to the different effect of these four keyboard instruments.

| Piano | Organ | Synthesiser | Harpsichord |

Two of the instruments have strings which are struck or plucked as the performer plays the keyboard. Can you name which two?

2 Unlike the piano or harpsichord, the next instrument, the guitar, has the strings directly beneath the fingers of the performer.
Listen to the recording.

| Classical Guitar (nylon strung) | Folk Guitar (steel strung) | Electric Guitar |

Decide which of these words best describes the sound of each instrument:
'metallic'
'breathy'
'distorted'
'mellow'
'brassy'

3   Percussion instruments are often grouped into recognisable combinations or families. Listen to the drums of the standard kit used in the many varied styles of popular music.

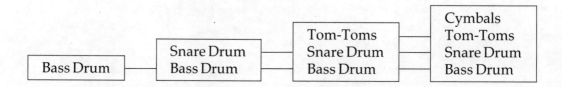

4   Congas, bongos, agogos, timbale and cabasa are frequently heard in music influenced by Latin-American styles. One of the sounds in the following recording is not a percussion instrument but is used to add to the excitement of the rhythm – can you spot it?

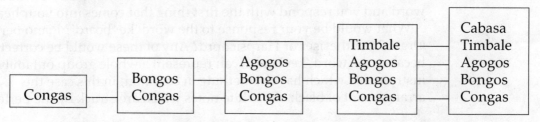

5   The descant recorder, often used in school music making, is also part of a larger family of instruments. Listen to this recording of a descant, treble, tenor and bass recorder playing together as a group or consort.

The sound is similar to one of the keyboard family heard in an earlier example. Can you suggest which instrument, and give any reasons why this might be?

6   Now listen carefully to the next three recordings and decide which *two* instruments are playing in each.

(a) Drum Kit	(b) Synthesiser	(c) Latin Percussion
Latin Percussion	Harpsichord	Classical Guitar
Electric Guitar	Recorder	Synthesiser
Piano	Electric Guitar	Pipe Organ

Light and shade 1

Listen again to the snare drum pattern you heard in *Beats and bars*. First it is played as it was before, but then it is repeated with some notes louder, some softer. These changes in volume or dynamics add variety.

Dynamics are an important element of musical expression. The changes can be sudden for a startling effect, or more gradual to control the tension or excitement of the piece.

Composers have long recognised the musical value of such effects, and indicate which passages are to be played softly or loudly with the Italian words *'piano'* or *'forte'*. For convenience the single letters *'p'* and *'f'* are used, with a very soft sound or passage marked *'pp'* or even *'ppp'* and a very loud sound or passage *'ff'* or *'fff'*.

1   The rhythmic pattern of the next recording is written below. Copy out the pattern and enter *'f'* or *'p'* in the boxes as appropriate.

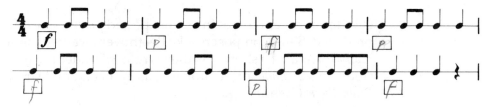

2   Sometimes a phrase will grow gradually louder or softer and is often marked with the following signs.

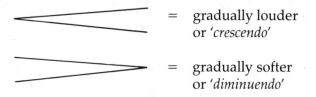

= gradually louder
or *'crescendo'*

= gradually softer
or *'diminuendo'*

Here are three 2-bar patterns played on the snare drum. Copy out the patterns and then listen carefully. When you have decided where each gets gradually louder or softer, write the correct sign underneath.

(a)

(b)

(c)

3 This rhythm gets both louder and softer. Mark it accordingly.

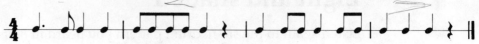

4 Look again at example 1. Most of the changes in dynamics occurred clearly on the first beat of the bar except in one bar where there was a *crescendo*. Listen once more and mark this bar with the correct sign.

5 So far we have heard regular dynamic variations and examples of *crescendo* and *diminuendo*. Sometimes, however, a single note will be accented for special effect. Copy out the following rhythm and then listen for any sounds which are stressed with an accent. Mark these with a > immediately above or below the note.

When an accent comes in an unexpected place a syncopated effect is produced. Some composers, like Beethoven, wanted the accents to be really forceful. To show this they wrote '*sf*' under the note, which stood for *sforzando*, or 'reinforced', as in this example from Beethoven's *Prometheus Overture*.

Listening test 1A

Answer all questions on the test sheet provided: questions 1–5 on or under the staves and questions 6–14 in the boxes at the foot of the page.

Read through the questions. Then listen to the recording. It will be played a number of times with an interval between each playing. As you listen, follow along the staves a bar at a time, pointing with your finger if this helps you to keep your place. A number of bars have been completed and as you follow, the music should be doing what the notes indicate in those bars. Try not to panic.

1   Add a time signature at the beginning.
2   Write the rhythm of bars 1 and 2 on the note F in the bass clef.
3   Complete the melody in bars 3 to 6.
4   Mark with an R the bar in which this 4–bar tune returns.
5   Add suitable dynamic marks in bars 1, 5 and 16.

6   The left-hand rhythm at the beginning is played on two notes at the same time. What is the interval?
7   What do you call a feature like this?
8   How many bars altogether have the same left-hand rhythm?
9   Are they all at the same pitch? If not, in which bar does the pitch change for the first time?
10   Does it go up or down?
11   When the tune returns for the first time, what is different?
12   What do *tranquillo* and *dolce* mean in bar 16?
13   Béla Bartók who wrote this piece was fascinated by numbers and their relationship. What in this piece relates to the numbers 6, 7 and 8?
14   The piece is called 'The Highway Robber'. Suggest a way in which the music illustrates the title.

Listening test 1B

Answer all questions on the test sheet provided: questions 1–8 and 12 on or under the staves and the remaining questions in the boxes at the foot of the page. Read through questions 1–10 and then listen to the first extract.

1 Add a suitable time signature.
2 Correct the bass drum part in bar 4.
3 Complete the melody in bars 6, 7 and 8 using a rest where necessary.
4 Add *f* and *p* in bars 9–12 to show where the music is loud and soft.
5 Complete the melody in bars 11 and 12.
6 Place an 'x' above the snare drum part where the high-hat cymbals are played.
7 Notate the rhythm of the tom-tom part in bars 14–16 adding accents as required.
8 Name the bracketed interval in bar 16.
9 Does the main tune sound as if it is played on a guitar, a xylophone, a recorder or a piano?
10 The melody in bars 11 and 12 is almost the same as that in bars 9 and 10. What is different?

Now listen to the second extract which is twice as long as the printed music.

11 How is the music lengthened?
   (a) by playing it more slowly?
   (b) by repeating each bar twice as it comes?
   (c) by repeating most of the tune exactly?
   (d) by doubling the length of each note?
   Put a circle round a, b, c or d on the test sheet.
12 In the first extract the music is unfinished. In the second, the music ends clearly. Write a capital D at the point where the melody you hear departs from the printed notation.
13 Describe the shape of the additional string synthesiser melody above the main tune.
14 What sort of percussion is added towards the end of the piece: bells and gongs, Latin-American percussion, or steel drums?

Level 2

Beats and bars 2

In Level 1 *Beats and bars* we looked at simple rhythms in $\frac{2}{4}$, $\frac{3}{4}$ and $\frac{4}{4}$ time, made up mostly of one-beat or half-beat notes and rests.

Some rhythms dwell on longer notes and often close on a note lasting a whole bar.

1 Listen to this recording of an old German folk tune. The melody is in $\frac{4}{4}$ time. How many times does the tune dwell on a minim or two-beat note? Be careful not to include the final note which lasts for the whole bar.

Now listen again and complete the notation below.

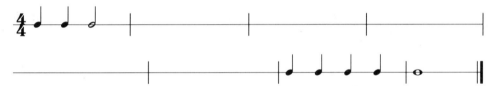

2 The next example, of Gospel style piano, has a very strong bass line moving along in dotted minims ♩. (three beat notes) bar by bar. Only in bars 3 and 7 does the pattern change to push the music along. Listen to the recording and decide which two of the following rhythms fits those bars.

3 Silence is a very important element in the creation of interesting and varied music and a rest sign is used to indicate where and how long any silence should be.

    𝄽 1 beat
    ▬ 2 beats
    ▬ 4 beats

Listen now to the following two-part piece. Complete the rhythm by adding stems and tails to the note-heads and inserting the correct rests.

4   In the next example, which is played twice, an electronic organ plays the chords of G and F major against a regular bass. The second time around the organ chords are delayed by a half-beat silence or quaver rest ♩. Sometimes the silences in the organ part are interrupted by short rhythmic clusters of chords. Can you spot how many times this occurs? A lot of Reggae music is based on this interplay of a solid bass line and offbeat chordal work.

5   Cowbell

Bass drum

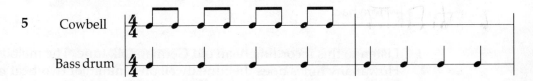

For every bass drum beat above there are two quaver taps on the cowbell, but in the second bar three taps are squeezed in – a 'triplet', written like this ♫♫ or this ♫♫ .

Listen to the recording and complete the cowbell rhythm adding the ♫♫ on the correct beat.

6   Triplets are often used in marching music to roll into the strong first beat of each bar. This acts as a signal to help those marching to keep in step or time.

Listen to a typical march-time pattern on the snare drum. Notice that it starts on an up-beat and notice also the way the triplets build to a climax towards the end. Complete the rhythm where notes are missing.

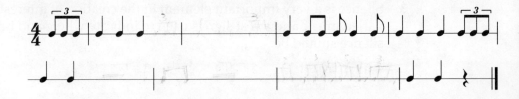

7   Triplets can also have a fanfare-like effect as in the introduction to this famous piece of music. Where might this music be performed and why? Can you name the composer?

Shapes and sizes 2

For a melody to be interesting it must have shape and variety. This is achieved in many ways. Earlier we listened to melodies which moved in steps. Now listen to these three tunes. The first is a trumpet call and uses these notes,

which come from the triad of B♭ major

The second is the tune of one of the best known arias from Mozart's *The Marriage of Figaro* which scrambles the notes of two chords into a catchy tune, with the help of some repeated notes.

And the third is the tune of *In the mood* which was made famous by Glen Miller's orchestra. Its jazzy chord shape pattern is repeated at three different pitch levels.

A♭   D♭   E♭

All three tunes jump from one chord note to the next, missing out one or two steps of the scale at a time. But the majority of melodies mix steps, jumps and repeated notes to create a pleasing sense of balance and shape, like this hymn tune, which opens with the notes of the chord of C major.

Notice the way the jumps get progressively wider as they go up and are balanced in the next two bars by the steps of a downward scale. Can you name the bracketed intervals?

Some melodies begin with steps before introducing jumps, like the German folk song *HoLaHi*.

Think of the theme music of the popular TV series EastEnders. Does this start with jumps or steps?

1   Listen to these tunes by Handel and Bach. Which pattern best describes each?

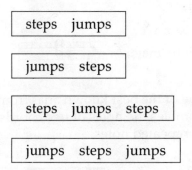

Sometimes a jump of an octave is used for melodic effect as at the start of *Over the Rainbow*. This tune mixes steps and smaller jumps as it continues.

2   Think through the tune of *Hot Cross Buns* and complete the first four bars of the melody.

3   Now listen to *My Love She's but a Lassie Yet* which starts like this.

How many times altogether does the downward octave jump occur? Is it always at the same pitch?

4 Follow the tune of *Linstead Market* as you listen to the recording. Notice that the first two lines are nearly the same, as are the next two. The first phrase of each pair of lines seems to open as if it wants to go on, the second phrase closes as if it has come to an end. Only a few notes are different.

Here are some more tunes which have phrases with open and closed endings. Copy them, listen to the recording and then complete the closing phrases.

Wata come a me y'eye (Jamaican)

(a)

Dorset four-hand reel

(b)

Jessie James (American)

(c)

Chords and cadences 2

A great many popular tunes and pieces are based on a few very simple chords. Of these, by far the most common are the chords built on I, the tonic, and V, the dominant.

Key C: I   V

The chord of V often has an extra note a seventh above the root. In this form it is known as the dominant seventh.

V   plus   7th above
root   becomes V_7

The dominant seventh pulls strongly towards the tonic chord and, at the end of a phrase, the two chords form a perfect cadence or full close. This is like a musical full stop.

V_7 I

The underlying harmonies strengthen the feeling of phrase structure. This is in contrast to a tune with a drone where the same bass continues throughout the piece.

Listen to the examples which will help you become familiar with the sound of a perfect cadence. Notice the way the bass moves, strongly, up a 4th or down a 5th.

(a)   Allegro   Haydn: String Quartet, op. 33 no. 5

Perfect cadence

(b)

Gilbert and Sullivan: *The Pirates of Penzance*

Perfect cadence

(c)   Rock cadence 1 *(JN)*

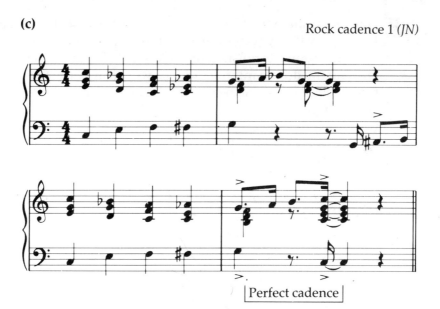

Perfect cadence

1 Now listen to six other examples. Three end with perfect cadences. These will sound as if they have finished. Three have other types of cadence which will not sound so final. Say which examples end with a perfect cadence.

(a) *Swing Low Sweet Chariot* (bars 1 – 4)

(b) *Swing Low Sweet Chariot* (bars 5 – 8)

(c) Corelli: Sarabanda

(d) Rock cadence 2

(e) Folk dance

(f) Dvořák: *American String Quartet*, third movement

Of the other cadences, the most important is called an imperfect cadence. At the end of a phrase, it sounds almost like a comma. It is sometimes known as a half close as the music does not sound as if it has ended. The *second* chord of an imperfect cadence is V. The first chord is sometimes I, but might be another chord like II or IV or even a chord from another key.

Key C: I   V   II   V   V₇ of V   V

2   Here is the melody of *The Prince of Denmark's March* by Jeremiah Clarke.
Follow it with the recording and at the end of each phrase ask yourself
whether it sounds finished or unfinished. Try to listen to the bass. If it
ends on the dominant, the cadence will be imperfect; if it ends on the
tonic, the cadence will be perfect. Write Imperfect or Perfect in the boxes
accordingly.

Groups and families 2

E 과피어I드그나나르
C D E F G A B C

In Level 1 *Groups and families* you heard instruments of the keyboard family, guitars, various percussion instruments and recorders. In this section you will hear music for strings, brass and woodwind. These three families, with their different characteristics, form the basis of the standard orchestra. The woodwind instruments, flute, oboe, clarinet and bassoon, along with their smaller and larger cousins like the piccolo and cor anglais, contribute a wide range of individual colour. The brass instruments, trumpets, trombones and tuba provide power and brilliance as well as marvellous sonority in soft and loud passages. The French horns, with their unique sound, blend well with these instruments and with the woodwind. The strings, which have a quite different quality, form the largest body of the orchestra, numbering as many as fifty players.

Each family of instruments is also heard frequently as a group on its own with just one player to a part. The four players in a string quartet play two violins, a viola and a cello. They produce a sound which is unified yet surprisingly varied.

1   Listen to the beginning of the last movement of Mozart's String Quartet in Bb K 458. Notice the way the four instruments vary the texture by sometimes playing alone, sometimes in pairs or threes and sometimes all together. Notice the way they pass ideas back and forth between each other, and how they contrast soft and loud passages.

When you have listened several times, complete the bar-plan of the first 32 bars by drawing a wavy line where the two violins play. Mark where the music is soft or loud with *p* or *f*. The music is in a quick two-time and the first violin plays by itself for two bars before the second violin and viola join in.

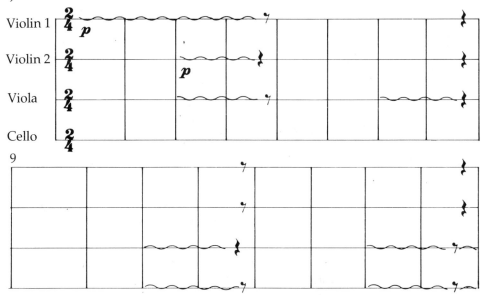

17

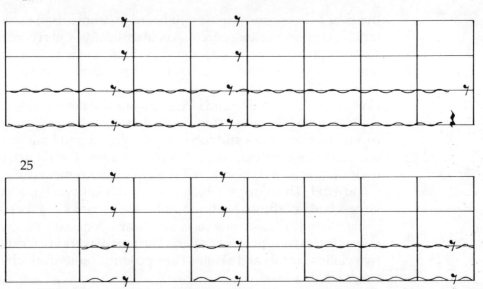

25

After bar 32, the last phrase is repeated a note lower, then the music continues in three parts until the cello enters for a series of loud, strong quaver chords on all four instruments. At this point, the texture is even denser, for the second violin plays in double stopping, i.e. two notes at a time. The chords end the extract with three rapid perfect cadences in C major.

2   A brass quintet usually has two trumpets, a horn, a trombone and a tuba. The players of these instruments can produce a sonority (especially when playing softly) which is smooth and rich and almost as well blended as that of a string quartet. But, in addition, they are able to use the individual qualities of each instrument to full effect to achieve great contrasts of colour, texture and dynamic range.

Listen to a section of Victor Ewald's Symphony for five-part brass choir. Notice the way the tune, which is in a slow $\frac{5}{4}$, is first played by a trombone

before being passed up first to one trumpet and then to the other. Notice, too, the way the instruments which are not playing the tune weave a web of sound round it. When you have listened a number of times to the extract, answer these questions about the music.

(a)   In the first few bars, does the first trumpet play mostly steps, chord notes, or repeated notes?

(b) How is the main tune extended when it is taken up by the first trumpet?

(c) How is the texture of the music changed after the climax?

(d) What happens in the last two bars?

A woodwind group has the greatest contrast in tonal quality. Each instrument has its own colour and characteristics which in part arise from the fact that the oboe and bassoon are double reed instruments, the clarinet has a single reed and the flute has no reed at all. Groups of woodwind players have to work very hard for the unified sound which is almost natural for brass and strings, and they are often joined by a French horn, which seems to help the blend. Music for wind ensemble often contrasts one colour against another.

3 Listen to the fourth movement of Geoffrey Winters' *Contrasts on a Theme from Liszt*, where the instruments of the wind quintet are thrown into sharp relief. Notice how they pass a three-note figure from one to another, and the way the horn's repeated notes, heard at the beginning, are later taken up by all the instruments.

When you have listened several times describe the music of the middle section which starts with an idea low down on the bassoon.

Light and shade 2

If you look back at the Haydn Quartet example on page 23 you will notice that Haydn not only contrasts *forte* passages with *piano* passages and four-part textures with solo (as well as sound with silence), but that he also contrasts the smooth *legato* of bars 5–6 and 9–10 with the short staccato sounds of bar 7.

In addition he carefully marks which notes in the first idea are to be slurred and which are to be played staccato.

Listen now to the way Mozart, in his G Major String Quartet, first announces a tune legato,

and then immediately presents a staccato variation,

followed by a further variation of the repeat.

As the music continues, it contrasts *forte* and *piano* and changes the texture as well.

Where no dots or other marks are added to the notes a player assumes that the music is to be played legato. Where slurs over two or more notes are written, wind players 'tongue' only the first note under the slur and string players play the notes 'in one bow' instead of bowing each note separately.

1 Now listen to some brass tunes which mix legato and staccato. Add dots above or below the notes which are short and staccato, and slur any pair of notes which sound joined. The first bar of each example is done for you.

Ewald: Symphony for five-part brass choir

(a)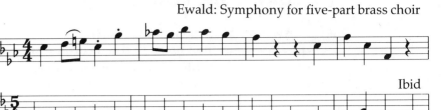

Ibid

(b)

Susato: Ronde

(c)

Beethoven:
Symphony no. 3

(d)

2 Here are three sets of identical tunes which are marked in different ways. Listen hard to the recording and then copy out the example in each set which matches the articulation used. Each example is repeated twice.

(a)

(b)

(c)

The articulation of a musical idea makes a great deal of difference to its character. Composers are careful to show just how their music is to be played. Performers must pay due attention to detail and not be careless.

3 Imagine now that you are helping a beginner on the recorder to play more accurately. Listen to the performance and put a cross against the music where it is played incorrectly. Listen for mistakes in articulation (staccato instead of legato) as well as for any wrong notes and rhythms.

Listening test 2A

Answer all questions on the test sheet provided. Read through the questions and then listen to the recording which will be played a number of times with an interval between each playing. The first extract is of the eight bars represented by the outline score, the second extract is of the whole section.

Use the outline score to show the following in an appropriate way.

1 The names of the four instruments playing.
2 The number of beats in a bar.
3 The articulation (slurs and staccato dots) in the first line.
4 The place where the melody should be marked *sf*.
5 The rhythm (or melody) played by the second instrument up to bar 2.
6 The rests the two lower instruments have before they enter for the first time.
7 The bass notes, or the name of the cadence across bars 3 and 4.
8 The melody of bars 5 and 6.
9 The passage in which the second instrument plays the same tune as the first an octave lower. Write the notes it plays or mark the bars with a wavy line.
10 The point at which the music is repeated.

Now listen to the whole extract and answer these questions in the boxes below the score on the test sheet.

11 How is the texture changed after the repeat?
12 After how many bars does the first tune return?
13 How is its presentation varied?
14 How do the last four bars differ from the music in bars 5–8?
15 Is this an extract from a trio sonata, a string quartet, a concerto grosso or a banjo band?
16 Who might have written this piece: J.S. Bach, Andrew Lloyd Webber, Haydn or Verdi?

Listening test 2B

Answer all questions on the test sheet provided: questions 1–7 on or under the staves and questions 8–16 in the boxes at the foot of the page.

Read through the questions. Then listen to the recording which will be played a number of times with an interval between each playing.

1 Complete the rhythm in bars 1 and 2.
2 Complete the melody in bars 5–8.
3 Add dynamic marks in bars 1 and 9.
4 Name the melodic intervals at the beginning of bars 9 and 10.
5 Which interval comes at the beginning of bar 11?
6 Add a suitable dynamic mark in bar 15.
7 Show with Roman numerals, or letter names, the two chords used in bar 16.

8 Which family of instruments is playing this piece?
9 Name the instrument which plays the top line.
10 Comment on the texture of the music.
11 Compare the melody in bars 1–8 with that in bars 9–16.
12 Listen hard to the bass part. Compare what it does in the first section with its movement in the second.
13 The upper instruments of this piece mostly move together in rhythmic unison. In which two bars do they not have exactly the same rhythm as each other?
14 Name the cadence in bar 16.
15 This piece is based on a once-fashionable dance. Is it a gigue, a sarabande, a waltz or a polka?
16 When might this piece have been written: in the 16th, 17th, 18th or 19th century?

Level 3

Beats and bars 3

In $\frac{2}{4}$, $\frac{3}{4}$ and $\frac{4}{4}$ the beat is a crotchet.

But any note value can be taken as the beat.

In $\frac{3}{8}$ it is a quaver.

In $\frac{2}{2}$ it is a minim.

And in $\frac{6}{8}$ the beat is a dotted crotchet and there are two such beats in a bar.

Times which use dotted beats are called compound times because the beat is compounded of a note and a dot.

Each beat divides into three quavers (like a triplet),

or unequally into a crotchet and a quaver.

   You will be very familiar with the sound of compound time for, from an early age, you will have heard it in nursery rhymes,

in folk songs,

and in the very famous jig, *The Irish Washerwoman*.

1 Listen to the recording. Then write out the rhythms you hear. They are all in $\frac{6}{8}$ and use ♩. or ♩ ♪ or ♫♩ only.

(a)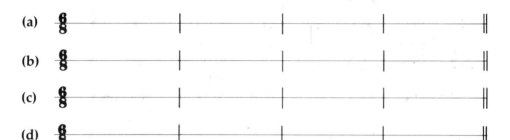

(b)

(c)

(d)

2 A rest may be substituted for either the crotchet or the quaver.

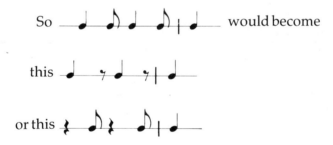

So ____ ♩ ♪♩ ♪|♩ ____ would become

this ____ ♩ ⅞ ♩ ⅞|♩ ____

or this ⅞ ♪⅞ ♪|♩ ____

But publishers differ in the way they write a one beat rest in compound time. Some write ⅞· . Others, more traditionally, use ⅞ ⅞ .

Listen to the recording and then write in the names of the two instruments which are playing. Then complete the upper part using one beat rests where necessary. The rhythm starts with a single quaver which is balanced in the last bar by the equivalent of five quavers.

3 A rhythmic pattern which occurs naturally in compound time is ♩. ♫ .
The first quaver is lengthened with a dot and the second is shortened to a
semiquaver. This figure is freely substituted in many folk tunes for equal
quavers to add variety and a lilt to the rhythm.

The melody of *Blow the Man Down, Bullies* is written here with plain
quaver groups. Listen to the recording and change any groups which are
sung with ♩. ♫ .

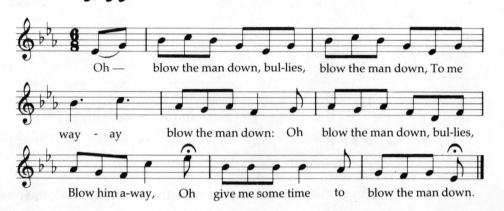

4 Now listen to two famous operatic tunes. They are both chord note
melodies and they both use the rhythmic pattern ♩. ♫ . Write out their
rhythms or continue their melodies.

Bizet: *Carmen*

Wagner: *Die Walküre*

5 The theme from the last movement of Haydn's String Quartet in G makes
great use of the rhythmic pattern you have been studying as you can see
from the first few bars.

Listen to the theme and then to the first variation which starts like this.

Shapes and sizes 3

1   The tune of the 19th-century song *A Life on the Ocean Wave* has remained popular ever since it was written and is often heard as a march. Like so many good tunes it is very simple. It is mostly made up of a stepwise figure plus groups of repeated notes. The stepwise figure is sometimes tipped upside down or inverted.

Listen to the tune, then slot the boxes into their correct places.

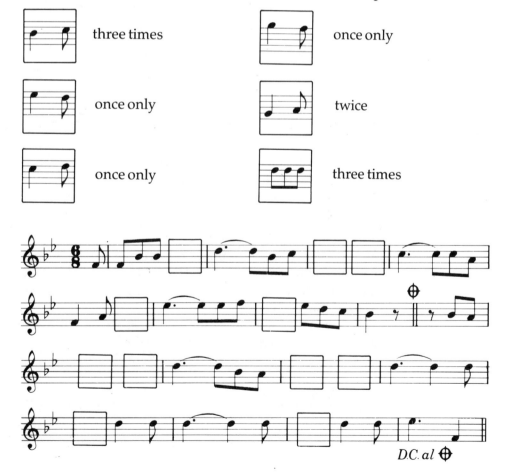

After the *da capo* repeat there is a Coda, or tailpiece, which starts like this. Write in the rest of the tune.

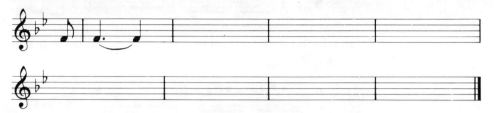

2   When it is not repeating the same note, *A Life on the Ocean Wave* moves mostly by step. The fiddle tune *Rattle the Cash* uses chord-note ideas mixed with repeated notes.

   Listen to the recording and then complete the melody.

   In the second section notice the way the first two bars are played a note higher in the next two bars. This device is called a sequence. If you look back at the Dorset reel on page 22 you will find another example of a sequence.

3   Sequences are found in many tunes especially in the second or middle sections. However the *Dargason*, which goes on and on without stopping, starts straight away with a 2-bar sequence which is cleverly changed in the second line with an octave jump.

   Listen to the recording and then complete the tune. It uses jumps, steps and repeated notes. Watch out for   .

4   In 1893 when the Czech composer Dvořák was visiting the USA, he not
    only wrote his most famous symphony, the ninth ('From the New
    World'), but also his American String Quartet. In both he shows the
    melodic and rhythmic influence of Negro and North American Indian folk
    music. One feature of these is the extensive use of the pentatonic, whose
    scale, when based on F, uses these five notes.

    Listen to a short extract from the start of the Quartet and notice the way
the largely chord-note tune uses just five different notes.

(a)   Can you hear which five different notes are used?
(b)   Why are they written in the alto clef?
(c)   What happens after these four bars?
(d)   What do the violins play before the first tune?

Chords and cadences 3

1   Here are some snippets from five well-known songs, all in the key of F.
    They are all based on the notes C D C which in solfa are the sounds soh
    lah soh. Copy the extracts, then listen to the recording and decide which
    snippet belongs to each tune. Write the words under the music.

2 If chords are added to these melodic fragments, the note C is usually given a tonic (or F) chord and the D a sub-dominant chord. This chord is formed on the fourth note of the scale and in the key of F is a B♭ chord.

(As you will see, the chord of V also contains the note C and is sometimes used in place of I.)

So *One more river* would be harmonised like this:

Key F: I   IV   I

When chord I follows chord IV at the end of a phrase they make a plagal cadence.

Key F: IV   I

Plagal cadences are much less common than perfect and imperfect cadences although they are found at the end of hymns and prayers, to the word 'Amen', where the top note often stays still.

Key F: IV   I

Listen now to an instrumental version of *For He's a Jolly Good Fellow*. The chord of IV comes six times, first in bar 2, then in bar 6. Where else is it used? Where is there a plagal cadence?

Did you spot the sequences? Where were they? Were they exact? Which cadence is used at the end?

3   The tune of *The Quaker's Wife* has perfect, imperfect and plagal cadences. The cadence points are marked below the music. Listen to the recording and name each cadence. For example, the cadence at (a) is imperfect as its second chord is V and the music does not sound finished.

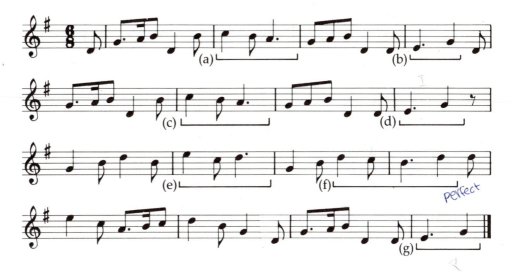

Groups and families 3

You have already heard examples of small groups of similar instruments playing together: a recorder consort, a string quartet, a brass quintet. These groups and families have a unity of sound which is easy to recognise and pleasing to hear. However, many of the most exciting instrumental combinations mix together instruments from several families, as for example in a rock group, where guitars, keyboards and drums are blended or contrasted with each other. Some mixed groups or ensembles have only a few members; some, as with a symphony orchestra or brass band, have many. In most groups, whether large or small, certain instruments usually play the top line, tune or melody, others are natural bass-liners, and yet others fill in the middle ground with supporting accompaniment or harmony. The tune may also turn up in the bass or in an inside part, whilst lead or melody instruments take over the job of keeping the rhythmic accompaniment going; this gives greater interest and variety for both players and listeners. As well as switching from one part to another, the main tune may be joined by counter melodies.

1   Listen now to *Rock Study One* and follow the instrumental structure plan as you do so. Notice how in section 1 bass and percussion set the mood, in section 2 the synthesiser joins in with middle ground harmonies before being joined, in section 3, by the lead guitar.

1	2	3	4	5	CODA
electric bass drums	synthesiser ⟶ ⟶	lead guitar ⟶ ⟶ ⟶	SILENT		

Describe what happens in section 4 where the percussion part is silent and in section 5 where all the instruments again join in. What happens at the end in the coda?

2   The Ian Houston Quintet is made up of two saxophones, piano, bass and drums. Sometimes, as in this extract from a jam session, one of the sax players helps out on an additional percussion instrument. Listen to the recording and then match the instruments to their musical contribution.

Instrument	Contribution
alto and tenor saxophone	ostinato rhythm
piano	backing rhythm
electric bass	rhythmic harmony
drums	lower part
additional percussion	tune in octaves

What was the additional percussion instrument: a triangle, cowbell, maracas or tambourine?

3   Like the rock group and jazz quintet, The Gainsborough Consort has two melody instruments, flute and violin, a keyboard instrument and a bass. When they play music of the baroque they use a viola da gamba (a leg viol), for the bass part instead of the cello. The keyboard and bass part together is known as a *basso continuo* (or just *continuo*), because together they play a continuous bass part under the melody instruments. In addition, the keyboard player fills in the harmony in the middle ground.

Corelli, who wrote much fine music for the violin in the days of the great violin maker Stradivarius, was also famous for his trio sonatas. Although played by four people these are essentially for two solo instruments and continuo. Listen carefully to the first few bars of the Gigue from the Trio Sonata in E minor.

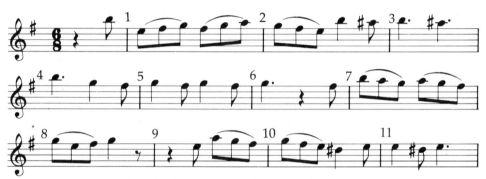

Now answer these questions:
(a)   Which solo instrument plays first?
(b)   Where does the second solo instrument come in?
(c)   Which instrument is this?
(d)   What does it play?
(e)   Which keyboard instrument plays the continuo part?
(f)   Where does the continuo imitate the first melodic idea?
(g)   Comment on the shape of the melody in bars 7 and 8.

Now listen to the whole movement. Notice:
(a)   the way the first vital idea is passed between the instruments including the continuo
(b)   how first one instrument and then another starts the conversation
(c)   the extension of the idea in the middle
(d)   the four soft chords on all the instruments together which interrupt the flow
(e)   the way, shortly after this, the two solo instruments play in parallel thirds, to be answered straightaway by the continuo on the second beat
(f)   the last chord

4   *The Galloping Major* was a popular music hall song which Gordon Jacob arranged for the comedy radio programme ITMA. The version in this recording has been transcribed for brass band by Geoffrey Brand who also conducts the Sun Life band.

Here is the start of the main tune.

Before it is heard there is a long introduction, using these elements:

horns and cornets (cup mutes)

A .... five times

cornets (straight mutes)

B .... twice

euphonium and baritone

C .... twice

solo cornet (open)

D .... three times

cornets

E .... once only

Listen to the music and then list them in the correct order starting like this:

| A | B | A | C | A | D | A | D | A | B | C | D | E |

What type of scale is used in B and C?

When the main tune arrives an unexpected instrument has been saved up for the repeated notes. What is it?

Now listen to the whole extract and enjoy the exhilarating music and performance. Notice, towards the end of the extract, the big *crescendo* on the ♩ ♪ ♩. figure which is repeated four times. What does it do besides get louder?

Light and shade 3

The sounds of all instruments can be modifed by playing them in special ways. The tone of a string instrument is changed greatly when a mute is clipped onto the bridge. When a composer wants this, the part is marked *con sordino* or *con sord.* By playing with the back of the bow a percussive effect is produced. When the player is to use the wooden back of the bow, the part is marked *col legno.* By playing close to the bridge, *sul ponticello*, a mysterious sound is produced. But by far the commonest way to change the sound of a string instrument is to pluck the strings with the fingers instead of using the bow. *Pizzicato* (or *pizz.*) is particularly effective on the cello where pizzicato chords can be spread upwards or downwards with the thumb or fingers. Occasionally when a composer wants to make you 'sit up' he asks for a snapped pizzicato where the string rebounds against the finger board. Bartók, who liked the sound of this effect, used this sign to indicate its use.

1   Listen now to the second movement of Paul Patterson's String Quartet which is played entirely pizzicato. Listen for the way the cello's first idea,

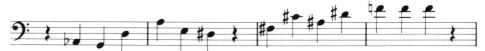

comes back in other forms, like this, in octaves on all four instruments,

and then, on the 1st violin over a march-like accompaniment.

Can you hear the way they are related?
   These three versions are found with others which make use of chords and of repeated notes. They are interwoven with a downward scale idea, sometimes in crotchets and sometimes in quavers. Which of these ideas is used to end the movement? Comment on the use of dynamics throughout the movement.

The tone of brass instruments can be changed considerably by the use of mutes. Mutes, which are inserted in the bell of the instrument, have been used since Haydn's day, but it is the influence of jazz musicians which has made them so popular today. They come in all sorts of shapes and sizes, but the most commonly used is the straight mute. The position of a cup mute is often adjusted whilst the instrument is being played. This gives a very special effect with the tone quality changing rapidly. Perhaps the most easily recognised is the wow-wow mute, which once it is heard, seems appropriately named. When a mute is to be used the part is marked *con sordino* or 'muted'. When the mute is to be taken out the part is marked *senza sordino* or 'open'. Sometimes the type of mute is clearly stated, as in *The Galloping Major*, which you heard in the last section, where the cornets who play repeated notes use cup mutes and the instruments which have the downward chromatic scales use straight mutes.

2   Listen now to Geoffrey Winters' *Mutations* for two trumpets. Follow the outline part and then mark where the different mutes are used. Notice that in some places one or other of the trumpets is left 'open'.

In recent years some composers have experimented with a great variety of tonal modifications to the sounds made by woodwind instruments. Flutter-tonguing, where the player rolls an 'r' to produce a form of trill, is now quite common. Other effects, like key tapping, bending the pitch and freely fluctuated overtones are less common. Of these new techniques, perhaps the most exciting is the ability to play more than one sound at a time on an instrument, like the flute, which normally plays just single notes. Such sounds are known as multiphonics.

3   Listen to part of Klaus Huber's *Ein Hauch von Unzeit I*, 'a complaint over the loss of musical reflection', which takes as its point of departure, the ground bass from Purcell's Lament from *Dido and Aeneas*.

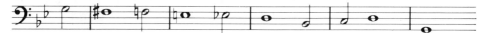

In this extract, the chromatic falling bass of the original is moved upwards by a series of trills, harmonics and multiphonics. Later in the piece Klaus Huber uses some of the other devices you have just heard.

Listening test 3A

Write your answers on the test sheet provided: questions 1–7 on or near the staves and questions 8–14 in the boxes at the foot of the page. The recording will be played a number of times with an interval between each playing.

1   Choose the most appropriate tempo marking from *Allegro, Largo, Moderato* or *Vivace* and write it in the correct place at the beginning.
2   Complete the melody of the first line adding stems and tails to the first few notes as necessary.
3   Mark with a cross the places in the second line where the melody is decorated.
4   Add the correct rhythm to the note-heads in bar 11.
5   Add slurs and staccato dots in bars 12–15 to show the way the music is played.
6   Add appropriate dynamic markings in the last two lines.
7   Complete the melody in bars 16–18.

8   Is this extract part of a string quartet, concerto grosso, trio sonata or flute concerto? Give reasons for your choice.
9   Which instrument plays the melody?
10   Which instrument doubles the melody?
11   Do the two instruments play mostly in octaves, 5ths, 3rds or 2nds?
12   Which two instruments play below the melody instruments?
13   Mention three features which add variety in the third line.
14   Mention two features of interest in the last six bars.

Listening test 3B

Answer all questions on the test sheet provided: questions 1–6 on or under the staves and questions 7–12 in the boxes at the foot of the page. Read through the questions and then listen to the recording, each extract of which will be played a number of times. The first extract is of the first verse and will be needed for questions 1–4 and 7–9.

1 Add a suitable time signature.
2 Complete the melody of the verse as far as the refrain.
3 Put circles round the notes which are sung in unison in the first refrain.
4 Name the cadence shown by the bracket in bars 11 and 12.
5 Add the key signature after the bass clef in the Instrumental break.
6 Complete the rhythm by adding stems and tails to the note heads.
7 The piece begins on C and F. What are the other note names used in the melody?
8 Which of these words describes a melody built on these notes, monophonic, pentatonic, canonic or philharmonic?
9 Is the first verse sung in two, three or four parts?
10 What is different about the arrangement of the second verse?
11 An electric guitar, on a slightly distorted setting, joins the accompaniment for the final verse. Listen carefully to its entry. Where has this rhythmic idea occurred before.
12 Mention two interesting features about the final refrain.

Level 4

Beats and bars 4

Here are the words of a famous English sea shanty.

> What shall we do with the drunken sailor,
> What shall we do with the drunken sailor,
> What shall we do with the drunken sailor
> Early in the morning?

Say them over in your head. Can you feel the accented words falling regularly like feet upon the deck as the anchor is hauled and wound up? Many shanties were work songs sung to relieve the drudgery of such a task, as well as to co-ordinate the effort of hauling and pulling.

1 **(a)** Here is the rhythm of the first line of *The Drunken Sailor*. Notice the two quaver–semiquaver patterns which fit the words in the first bar.

The rhythm is the same in the second and third lines but the fourth line is different. Copy out the words and add the rhythm above them.

(b) Each verse of the song ends with the refrain 'Hooray and up she rises'. In this the rhythmic pattern ♪. ♪ is introduced, stretching the first quaver (remember a dot makes the note half as long again), and shrinking the second.

    Look carefully at the two-bar pattern below, which has been printed without the ♪. ♪ pattern. Say the words in time and add a dot and semiquaver tail where the pair of quavers needs to be changed.

(c)   Here now are the words of verses 2, 3 and 4. Add their rhythms using these patterns:

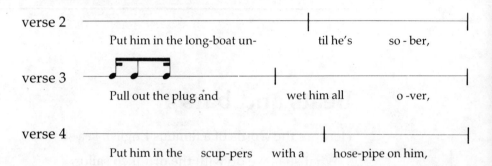

verse 2   Put him in the long-boat un-   til he's   so - ber,

verse 3   Pull out the plug and   wet him all   o -ver,

verse 4   Put him in the   scup-pers   with a   hose-pipe on him,

2   Listen now to the start of Robert Farnon's brass band piece *Bandutopia*. Notice the number of times he uses ♫ in the introduction before the solo cornet tune enters over an um-pa um-pa accompaniment on horns and basses. Listen carefully to that tune so that you can add its rhythm to these noteheads. Add slurs and staccato dots where necessary.

Now listen to some more of the music. Complete the structure plan by slotting in the labelled boxes A B C D in the correct order.

Introduction on cornets using ♩ ♫

?

Solo cornet tune

?

Sequence based on

?

Jaunty tune on cornets and horns

?

First tune back again an octave lower on euphonium and other instruments

A   Jaunty tune on trombones ending with syncopated glissandi

B

C   Um-pa um-pa accompanying idea on horns and basses growing louder and softer.

D   Tune on all cornets, played more loudly and extended with more ♫♩ figures

Shapes and sizes 4

Most well-known tunes are in the major, but some, like *What Shall We Do with the Drunken Sailor*, are in a mode and others, like *Charlie is My Darling*, are in a minor key.

A mode uses the same notes as a major scale but starts on a different rung of the ladder. This gives rise to different melodic shapes which revolve round other notes of the scale. Imagine yourself in the front coach of a train. To walk through the train from here you can go in one direction only before returning to your seat.

Now imagine yourself in the second coach. From here you can walk both towards the rear of the train and, for one coach, forwards.

Even though the eight coaches remain the same, your view of them is different.

If you compare sitting in the front coach with the scale of C

Scale of C

then being in the second coach is like the Dorian mode which starts on D.

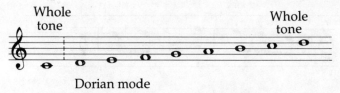

Dorian mode

It uses the same notes but now its final note is D and the note below this (which is C) is a whole tone away. The whole tone between the final note and the note below is characteristic of several modes. Listen out for it.

1 Here is an outline of the verse of *What Shall We Do with the Drunken Sailor*, which is in the Dorian mode. Think it through in your head and then fill in the missing notes.

2-bar sequence

2 The battle tune from Kodály's *Háry János* is also in the Dorian mode. Listen to it and then rearrange the eight bars into the correct order.

The shapes in minor tunes arise from the smaller-sized intervals between the tonic and third, and the tonic and sixth notes of the scale.

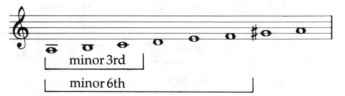

Some minor tunes, particularly from Eastern Europe, make use of the augmented 2nd between the sixth and seventh notes,

but more often than not this interval is smoothed out by raising the sixth note as well, as is done with the ascending form of the melodic minor scale.

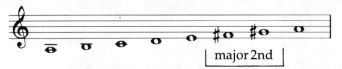

If this adjustment is made the scale sounds just like a major scale except for the important minor 3rd between the first and third notes. Descending melodic minor scales lower both the 6th and 7th notes to their natural position creating an Aeolian mode with a whole tone between the eighth and seventh notes.

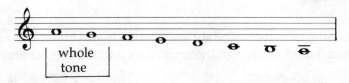

3   Think through the refrain of *Charlie is My Darling* and add the melody above the words in the key of C minor. It uses the rhythmic pattern ♩. ♪ many times.

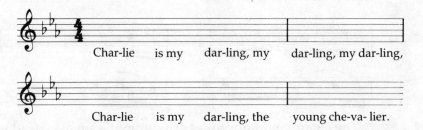

Now look at the verse and add natural signs where necessary in the first line, to raise the sixth and seventh notes of the scale.

4   Paganini was a virtuoso violinist and composer of the early 19th century. The theme from his *Caprice* in A minor has been used many times, by other composers, for sets of variations. It is ideal for this as it has a clear phrase

structure with strong sequences in the second part.
  Listen to the recording and complete the missing bars.

Chords and cadences 4

As with major tunes, melodies in the minor are often built on simple chord progressions with the chords of I and V strongly featured. As would be expected, the tonic chord in a minor key is a minor triad.

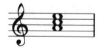

A minor: I

But, perhaps surprisingly, the dominant chord is usually major. Its middle note, or 3rd, is raised a semitone with an accidental to become the leading note of the scale.

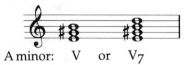

A minor: V   or V_7

  The first part of the Paganini theme you heard in the last section can be harmonised with just I and V like this.

I   V   I   V

As the tune goes on it slips into other keys for the sequences before returning to A minor.

Tunes which are in a mode are often built on chords which are a tone apart. Look again at *What Shall We Do with the Drunken Sailor* where the first chord, D minor, side-steps down to a chord of C major.

Here the chord of C major is the chord of VII in the Dorian mode. It is built on the seventh note of the mode, which is a whole tone away from the final note.

This side-stepping progression is characteristic of much folk music in both modal and minor keys. In a minor key it is often followed by an imperfect or a perfect cadence using the chord of V with the usual raised leading note.

1   Here are two folk dance tunes. They are both in two-time with a good number of beats dividing into four equal notes. But to make the page look 'less black' they are written out in $\frac{2}{2}$ time which has two minim beats in a bar. Copy them out, then listen to the recording. Decide where the chords change and write their names above the tunes.

   (a)   The first tune, *The Old Grey Cat*, used the chords of E minor, D and B7. Some chords last for two bars.

(b) The second tune, *Gilderoy*, uses mostly A minor, G and E7, but in the third line slips in a chord of C for a bar and half. Listen carefully for the places in which the chord changes on the second beat of the bar.

2 Listen now to part of an *Interlude* for flute, violin and harpsichord by Jacques Ibert. Like so much music written by French composers it has a Spanish flavour. The extract starts with a recitative-like passage on the violin before the harpsichord plays this figure,

which it repeats, with little change, for a good number of bars. Then, in bar 11, the left-hand part side-steps down a note to start the pattern on G, before descending further to reach E in bar 15.

Follow the flute part as you listen and then answer these questions.

(a)   What does the violin do when the flute has long notes in bars 3 and 7?
(b)   How is the melody varied in the second line?
(c)   How is the melody made richer in the third and fourth lines?

Now listen on to the end of the movement.
(d)   What does the violin do when it takes over from the flute?
(e)   Describe what happens after the music almost stops.
(f)   Comment on the flute and violin parts from this point.
(g)   How does the music come to an end?

Groups and families 4

Singing was possibly the earliest way of making music and it is still as enjoyable as ever. As with instruments, voices have their own particular colour – light, harsh, dark, nasal, clear, vibrant – and what may be considered a pleasing tone for one type of music, or in one country or culture, may be thought quite out of place in another. Voices too have different ranges and may be grouped together in many ways. The table below is a guide to the range of an average choral voice. Trained, solo voices may extend these ranges considerably up or down and in addition may have particular vocal qualities. For example, a coloratura soprano has a very flexible voice able to execute trills, scales and ornaments rapidly, whereas a dramatic soprano has a more powerful vocal style and a soubrette has a rather pert, light-hearted manner.

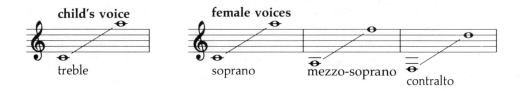

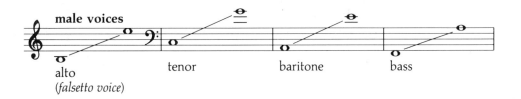

The various voices may be grouped in numerous ways, for example, two sopranos and an alto, or two tenors and two basses. In a pop or a madrigal group there may be just one voice to a part, whereas a large choral society choir may have more than a hundred sopranos singing just the top line. Sometimes all the voices will sing the same music in unison: at other times each voice will sing a different part in harmony. Then each part might have the same rhythm or might be quite independent. When you listen to vocal music try to decide which voice or voices are singing and whether one, few, several or many voices are singing each part. Ask yourself whether they are singing in unison or harmony and in the same or independent rhythms.

1   Listen to the end of Act 1 of Gilbert and Sullivan's *The Pirates of Penzance*, where the pirates have agreed to give up the opportunity to marry the Major-General's daughters. The extract starts with a brief introduction on the strings before the voices enter over repeated chords.

Notice that for ease of reading the music is written in *alla breve* or $\frac{2}{2}$ time with two minim beats in a bar.

Listen carefully to the next eight bars and then add the rhythm above the words in $\frac{2}{2}$ time. Use crotchets, quavers and crotchet rests. The barlines are given to help you.

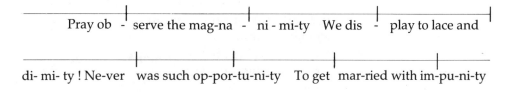

When you have checked the rhythm, rewrite it in $\frac{2}{4}$ in notes of half the length. Use quavers, semiquavers and quaver rests. Compare the look of the two versions and decide which you think is easier to read. They will both sound the same.

Now listen to the whole extract and describe what you hear. Think about the following when giving your answer.

> Do the girls or pirates sing first?
> Do they sing in unison or harmony?

> What do you notice about the rhythm when males and females sing together?
> Do they sing in unison or harmony?

> Do all the voices sing the same rhythm all the time?

> The orchestra ends the extract as the curtain comes down. How does its music relates to the rest of the extract?
> The passage is built on just three chords; can you say which and write out the progression?

> As often happens in opera, applause drowns the end of the music. Are there any other sounds that indicate that this is a recording of a live, amateur production?

2   Listen to *We Were Gathering up the Roses in the Wild Wood*. Is it sung by female, male or mixed voices? Most of the lines are sung in four-part harmony, but some are sung by a solo voice and some by a number of voices in unison. Follow the words and then copy out the lines which are not sung in harmony in two lists headed 'solo' and 'unison'.

> We were gathering up the roses in the wild wood,
> All on a merry summer day,
> And it's one more kiss before we part,
> Where the roses bloom so gay,
> Tiddily-um.
> Oh the look she gave to me,
> Rum-te-tum, te-tum, te-tum-ti, tiddily-iddily-um.
> Oh the look she gave to him,
> Rum-te-tum, te-tum, te-tum-ti, tiddily-iddily-um.
> We were gathering up the roses in the wild wood,
> All on a merry summer day,
> And it's one more kiss before we part,
> Where the roses bloom so gay.
> Tiddily-um.

3   Now listen to part of John Wilbye's *Adieu Sweet Amaryllis*. This is a
madrigal for mixed voices whose parts imitate each other as they take it in
turns to share the musical ideas. When you have listened a number of
times, complete the alto and bass parts of the first few bars.

Light and shade 4

Electronic treatment of sound

Imagine, it's your job to set up the percussion instruments for this week's
lesson and as you gather up the assorted sticks and beaters you cannot
resist trying the snare drum in the corner of the stock room. The chances
are it would sound something like this.

Now imagine that the lesson is to take place in the hall and as monitor
you are the first to arrive. Hit the snare again. It would sound something
like this. A much bigger sound, created by the thousands of echoes
bouncing off the walls, ceiling, radiators, indeed any reflective surface
creating natural reverberation. Although the sounds you have just heard
could have been recorded 'on location', they were, in fact, created
electronically with a small black box in a room no larger than our
imaginary stock room in the first example.

So, what else can we do with our box of tricks? At the flick of a switch
we can sound like two people talking at the same time, or a solitary
conversation up in the mountains ('Hello, wonderful echo up here!'). Or
perhaps record just one word and repeat all or part of it. This is a
technique called sampling. Or, why not alter the sound of a voice beyond
all recognition. The possibilities are endless!

Many composers have for a long time used electronic manipulation of
sound to create different and often startlingly original compositions, but it

is in the field of pop and rock music that these effects distinguish music of the 1980s from that of previous decades.

Let's take a closer listen to some of the current 'in vogue' effects.

Gated reverb.

Remember our 'snare drum in the hall' sound? Excessive use of this effect could literally smother the music in uncontrollable reverberation, so why not allow the reverberation to begin and then cut it dead or 'gate' it rather than allow the sound to decay naturally. Listen carefully to your favourite dance records; you may well spot the same effect.

Double tracking or Harmonising

The interval can be wide, as in our previous example of two people talking, or very narrow, to give the impression of someone singing along with him- or herself.

Echo or Delay

An echo need not take as long as the sound bouncing off our imaginary mountain. It could be very short and applied to an instrumental sound.

Sampling

The stuttered repeating of words is only one of the applications of sound sampling. Sound effects from any source can be recorded and incorporated in situations that would be difficult to recreate 'live' continually, e.g. smashing glass, gunshots, even a stab of orchestral sound!

1   Now listen to *Rock Study Two,* with vocals, guitar, synthesiser, bass and drums. During the course of the piece you will hear the following effects; list them in the order they occur.

A	Double-tracked vocal		D	Echoed synthesiser

B	Sampled orchestral stabs		E	Gated reverb. on snare drum

C	Echoed vocal

☐ ☐ ☐ ☐ ☐

2   Many modern composers use electronic techniques to create exciting collages of sound. Such pieces seldom have readily identifiable tunes or harmonic and rhythmic passages, but often have sound images and ideas which can be easily recognised as the music grows.

For example, listen in the next piece for these elements,

chattering cascades
climactic clashes
metallic twirlings
repetitive tapping
a sustained single note
zing-tonk motifs

which occur in pairs in each of the four sections.

When you have listened to *Malabar Moods* which is based on
a sustained pulsating drone, complete the pairings in the four boxes.

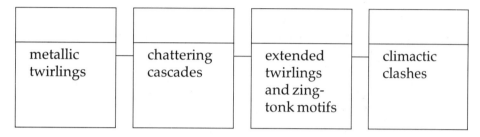

| metallic twirlings | — | chattering cascades | — | extended twirlings and zing-tonk motifs | — | climactic clashes |

Listening test 4A

This test is taken from Act 2 of Gilbert and Sullivan's *The Pirates of Penzance*, where the local constabularly sing of the way they bolster up their courage in the face of danger. The extract will be played a number of times.

1   After an introduction in which the police-force tramps on, a series of repeated chords of C leads to the Sergeant's melody. Complete the Sergeant's melody on the test sheet given, writing in the bass clef. The chorus line is complete and will help you to follow the music.

2   In the first twelve bars of this extract Sullivan uses just three chords.

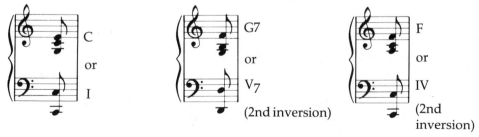

Each chord lasts for at least a bar, or as at the beginning, for several bars. Show where the chords change by writing their names, either above (C G_7 F), or below (I V_7 IV) the music.

Write your answers to the following questions in the boxes provided.

3 What happens to the rate of chord change in bars 13 to 16?
4 Is the Sergeant a bass, baritone or tenor?
5 Which voices sing the chorus line: female, male or mixed?
6 Describe the introduction and relate its features to the music of the solo and chorus lines.
7 What happens after the Sergeant's solo? Listen to the orchestral accompaniment, and to the bass line on instruments and lower voices.

Listening test 4B

The extract for this test is taken from Stuart Johnson's suite for brass band, *The Golden West*. The first movement, 'On the trail' is based on the traditional American tune, *Home on the Range*, which is in triple time and starts like this.

The version for brass band is in a swingy four time.

1 Complete the melody on the test sheet provided, writing it an octave higher than it sounds as played by the horns and baritones.
2 When you have completed the melody, follow the music further and answer these questions in the boxes provided.
  (a) As the horns die away do the cornets enter in *2nds*, *3rds*, *5ths* or *octaves*?
  (b) The horns soon return with *repeated notes*, *a chord tune*, or *an upward scale*?
  (c) They are followed by *a downward scale on the timpani and triangle, the soprano cornet* or *the euphoniums and baritone*?
  (d) Then the cornets continue the tune with *repeated notes, octave jumps* or *swooping glissandi*?
  (e) They are doubled an octave lower by *trombones, horns* or *basses*?
  (f) Then the basses play a link back to the first tune

like   or   or
this   this   this?

3 Describe some of the ways in which Stuart Johnson sets the mood of this piece.